Beasts & Violins

Beasts & Violins

poems by

Caleb Barber

Caleb B [signature]

Red Hen Press | *Pasadena, CA*

Book design by Mark E. Cull
Book layout by Sydney Nichols

Library of Congress Cataloging-in-Publication Data
Barber, Caleb, 1983-
  Beasts & violins : poems / by Caleb Barber.—1st ed.
    p. cm.
  ISBN 978-1-59709-469-6
  I. Title. II. Title: Beasts and violins.
  PS3602.A7594B43 2010
  811'.6—dc22
                    2009045119

The Annenberg Foundation, the James Irvine Foundation, the Los Angeles County
Arts Commission, Department of Cultural Affairs, Los Angeles,
and the National Endowment for the Arts partially support Red Hen Press.

First Edition

Published by Red Hen Press
Pasadena, CA
www.redhen.org

ACKNOWLEDGMENTS

The following poems appeared previously in these fine journals: *Alien Sloth Sex*: "Dear Old Dads;" *Best American Poetry 2009*: "Beasts and Violins;" *Cascade*: "To the Man Driving I-5 with a Rabbit on His Shoulder;" *Forge*: "Pace;" *Fulcrum*: "Bellingham's Favorite Son," "Camping with Mad, Far from Montana," and "False Eulogy for the Stillagaumish River;" *High Desert Journal*: "An Upstream Tow as an Early Date;" *Jeopardy*: "Report" and "Tavern Woman;" *Los Angeles Review*: "The Blue Collar Artist;" *Makeout Creek*: "Heart Lake: or, Poem for the Mistaken Boy;" *New Orleans Review*: "Twilight Town" and "What All Foxes Know (Two Ways Out of Their Burrows);" *Plain Spoke*: "Teaching the Beasts;" *Poet Lore*: "Beasts and Violins," "Black Omen," "The Buck," "Into Days Between Snow," "The False Twin," "The Fair Kaleetan, Between Friday Harbor and Anacortes," "Old Savage," and "Over Breakfast;" *Raven Chronicles*: "Captain Fidalgo;" *Portland Review*: "This Southwestern State;" *Rattle*: "I Went in with My Hands Up;" *Stringtown*: "Machined Parts to Monroe;" and *Soundings*: "Blue Stilly."

Also, I'd like to thank the following people: Stephanie and Harley Barber, Rijl Barber, Isaac Boyle, Rachel Mehl, everyone at the Northwest Institute of Literary Arts and Red Hen Press, Carolyne Wright, David Wagoner, and Tess Gallagher.

CONTENTS

II

III

Beasts & Violins

I

The False Twin

The dead man waits with the bear in its cave and the rabbit in its hutch in the snow.
—Marvin Bell

When I was born, the delivery room was still
for the baby being birthed dead
behind the curtain, beside my mother.
The doctors had been aware of it for weeks,
and so had its parents, after
the ultrasound had demonstrated
no heartbeat. But it's supposed to be
easier if these things are brought full term,
and the woman was induced
to labor, that late-August night
with the half moon drifting in Gemini.

So I'm told it was difficult
finding someone to wipe the froth
from my fresh shoulders and hand me back
to my dad, because the nurses
were all distracted, and the doctors
were all occupied with the silent
procedure in the next cell.
It is more complicated to receive
what has no cause to come
than what is unwilling to wait.

There are borders on the requirements
of death, and that blue baby
was shown every consideration.
His leaden life was given one audience,
and no call for hunger. And a ghost
must have incurred some sort of need
to need appeasement for it.
It should not be suggested

any puff of his spirit, when he slipped
cold from that hole, entered the other
birth in that room, for such a thing
would be too dark—it could not be contained.

Dear Old Dads

I've been making weekly trips
to the sanitarium,
and telling all the whackos
I'm their son.
They're so generous
—they fix every game of checkers we play,
pretending they know nothing
of kings.   Then they tighten the laces on my shoes,
admire my well-scrubbed face,
and offer half their juice.

When I stand to leave, they spit
pyramid-shaped pills
into my hands, and say,
"Boy, I've been saving these for you.
Swallow all of them
when your hair   starts to grow out,
and your eyes wander
toward shadows of buildings.
When you see a tractor,
and it's a rhinoceros
with taillights for eyes."

BLACK OMEN

"Tonight we suffocate the hive
—spray a can into the nest
until all they can breathe is poison.
We'll see the yellow jackets tumble out
stupid and shocked like dental patients
waking to find all their teeth
replaced with screws. Let's watch them
grovel across the porch slats
while they die, hundreds of bodies
becoming curled strips of whittled wood
waiting to be swept up.

"For days, far travelers will return,
circling the empty beam in confusion,
finally back from long journeys for the queen,
filled with juice of flies and caterpillars.
But her majesty's fat body
will have burst, after we've beaten the kingdom
with a shovel. She'll be just another mess
in the trash, and they'll have nowhere to go
but out back if they want to stick her
together again. If they want to hoist her
corpse on a twig and rebuild.

"Tonight there is a death on the house.
If your grandparents were visiting
their hearts would quit in their sleep.
You know the power's been shut off?
All the fridge meat is rotting.
I'm happy your mother is out of town.
Stay here a while with me, son. Help me
finish off these wasps. You don't have to go

to bed just yet. Tonight, even that broken-winged crow
you keep caged in that cardboard box
will be killed by the cat."

OLD SAVAGE

My mother, six months after
and dealing with a sabotaged estate,
told me about helping Georgia
out of the bathroom. Lifting her.
From tub or toilet I don't know.
Don't know the scene, the detail.

I know my grandmother looked
like a speckled heathen.
And beautiful. Hair long but always
braided. Face splotchy with brown
from liver spots, thyroid drugs, and gardening.
Plus some Indian blood that saved itself
for old age. Large cheeks. A smile
I only knew from when she was around
strangers or playing cards.
Those tissues stuffed between buttons
on a red flannel work shirt. Restless brow.

Lifting, my mother said to her,
there in the bathroom
(Georgia's chest had gone bad
and she suffered great faintness):
"Momma, you know I would
give you my heart if I could."

And my mother said to me,
in the truck on the freeway:
"And she looked at me, stopped
and really looked at me.
And she would have taken it."

PACE

With his body watching me
from the deck,
I dig a grave for Pace.
Dead this morning
beneath a rhododendron, I drove
my mother's car to him.
A favor—he was not mine.

It took all afternoon,
though it was warm,
peeling through the river clay
of the courtyard.   My leather gloves
fell apart as I went,
so when it came time to drag him to his plot,
I used my hands.
Pace was slick to touch.
He had been hosed off, yet maintained
all we won't say
about a raw corpse.

Still, it is hard to be respectful
when his Doberman legs,
liver-colored with blonde socks,
are so set, I have to shove them against his chest
until the joints *pop*,
so they won't stand out
from the soil.

False Eulogy for the Stillaguamish River on the Day of Gerald Ford's Funeral, 1/02/2007

This river drifted nuggets of alpaca dung
through the pastures at Darrington,
and a hundred years ago, bobbed with scores
of dogfish fins and entrails from canneries'
newfangled Iron Chink salmon processors.
This river sank 67 miles from the Cascades
to the Sound, and was not a strong brown god,
but gray and capacious. Rather than Hindu ashes,
the Stillaguamish would have born the distended corpses
of raccoons and deer, each twitching with parasites,
like demonic ice cubes, on their long float.

Rabbits have no tail and a river has no ass.
Rivers have only headwaters and mouth.
This river smelled of sun on snow, filtered
through peat. It obscured my hands with silt.
Go further, and it knew the fastest way
to separate a body from its brain.

Those who still consider the river are truant,
since a river is only a frontier for a little while.
I sang to the river from the reverb chamber
beneath a steel girded bridge. I played
my melancholy as if it were a theremin,
without touch. But the river thrummed me
like an electric bass. I had a lover who took pictures
of herself in different outfits all day long.
Rivers the world over grieved her.
Even the San Pedro, down in County Cochise,
that didn't even know which way to run.

No one will discuss today whether or not
this river was a hero. Whether or not
it made great sacrifice for the nation's good.
We can't claim to know a river's metabolism
—how reasonably it processes its own contribution
or demise. It rolls below our dull processions
daily, each morning it would have us don black.

What else can be said about a river,
other than that the rocks it hauled
became smooth, that it was accommodating
to rain, and that the gulls,
where it joined the sea, were fair?

This is a false eulogy. Today is not the funeral day
for a river. But from the interstate,
I saw it behind glass. It registered interred:
perfect in a clay casket, a drainage ditch
to stark new year's fields. The river's level
was down after weeks of storms, and people
had stopped worrying about it. The radio
had moved on. Trees grew from ground again
and even the mountains up the valley

appeared refined. But below the bridge
at mile post 209, the Stillaguamish is not dead.
This river sleeps to viola reveries,
drags its glory. And anyway, a river
can never flood. A river can only reclaim.

ADDRESSING A MONTH OF GUILT, DRIVING
NEAR THE CAMANO ISLAND EXIT OF INTERSTATE 5

The sign was up before the lodge was built:
Casino, with a red arrow aimed east.
Bulldozers wrecked the woods, shoving the base
of the timber with slow diesel force.
Roots shook their clods off as they tipped
blind into the gray of the winter hillside.

If the crew used chainsaws, I didn't
see them, but I know there is a certain beauty
to a Cat. If you like the smell
of slash piles burning in rain and the look
of smoke mixed with wakes of fast-moving cars,
you may find consolation even here.

REPORT

Meeting Ryuji on the way back from the chief's house
just after they had buried the cat was pure bad luck.
—Yukio Mishima

I won't tell my friend I read the book he loaned me,
beside the toilet, sick with flu.
But something like seasickness set in
when I started it, sometime
after midnight last Monday.
This incestuous 60's Japanese novel,
The Sailor Who Fell from Grace with the Sea
—a "masterpiece of taut violence"
according to the jacket, "Dense in substance,
far-reaching in allusion," says *Nation*.

My bowels a broken faucet, my mouth
a horror flick (certainly whatever
was coming out of me could not
be considered "dense in substance,"
and you wouldn't want to know
why the cat needed burying),
I finished and felt alright enough
to quiver on my back and discover
new patterns in the bathroom ceiling.

CAPTAIN FIDALGO

I'm pissing outside the gate again, aiming
at the bases of nettles where they lean
on red brick ballasts at the property's edge.
Only two horses and one molting mule
are around to watch, the horses sinking
bit by bit into pasture soil, the mule
mostly scaled now, dermal, like a diseased,
wingless griffin shaking tufts off into breeze.

Past the gate, the road runs in reverse
up the hill. It heads toward a large house
with steel hawk statues on each stump
throughout the exactly trimmed lawn.
It all cost money, and I know
the owner has it. I see the invoices
when I bring his parts, aluminum plates
to replace glass windows on planes.
Fuselages made lighter, requiring
less fuel to fly, but now lacking
any passenger views. Still, the plugs sell.

Anyway, I piss outside this man's gate
each time I drive to his island, though
he isn't such a bad man. He's English,
helps me unload, and even allows
his show-quality retriever to wander
through overgrowth the mule hasn't eaten.

But I don't trust his dual fortress.
This island outpost complete with compound.
Or that when I piss on the nettle stems
where they lean against the red brick ballasts

of the gate, I can't see the mansion
between the trees. If I could, I wouldn't
piss here. I'd have to ask to use his toilet,
and he might even let me, as long
as I would remove my boots first.

Still, I can't put faith in a man who conceives
of a cost-effective way to get airlines
to block over cabin windows.
Hell, I don't trust his mule.
Its fat grows in cylinders along its haunches
and neck, like a tumor of worm
with several bodies but a single head
too tangled to find.

CRAFT ISLAND HUNTERS WRECK THE DAY,

reclined against rocks before the sand-spread
of an estuary at low tide.
Their boots are soiled from the crossing,
but their shotgun stocks are dry,
nested in the illustrated wood-growth
of the two men's reinforced laps.

They appear as forgotten statues
from a lost war, with facial hair
that could only have been carved
from descriptions in historical fiction.
Were this island not so well visited
in the good months, it would seem
they could be tipped—each man pouring out
into dust over lichen pads, leaving
only husks to knock in the breeze.

They could have been sitting upright,
drying out there for decades, keeping vigil
for cannibal tribes that would ford
the narrows from separate island outposts,
after an apocalypse everyone else missed.
For now, no bird could match the pair
with orange shoulders, so it's good
none are around, and that the voles in the grass
offer no meaningful source of meat.

Except the clouds have gone
a forbidden white, the shallow waters
a nuclear green. No planes
have passed for hours,
from that county strip up the coast.

So at least let the Craft Island hunters
be kind. Let them offer a spare weapon,
when the makeshift canoes appear
with little dead girls for figureheads on the strait.

MACHINED PARTS TO MONROE

I stop off in buildings where the sinks
have all been yanked from the walls,
and the toilets are covered
in a fine gray silt. Constant trains
close the highway behind me
like an automatic gate.
At one warehouse compound
there are fifty doors in a U-shape,
with a car park in the center,
but none of the doors are ever open
and there is never a soul in the lot.
I stand in the rain and knock.

When someone answers, smoke chugs
from the dark and I step past
water buckets full of butts, to hand over boxes
for signatures. The parts roll away
on a conveyor into the green light
at the back of the shop,
to be plated or powder-coated.
I take my clipboard and go.

The fields in winter are a backwater lake
too shallow to be piloted.
Driving the highway, I see the only new things
are dents in the guard rails,
because the placement of the speed cops
never changes. Wherever I stop,
the crapped-out van leaks
red transmission fluid onto snow,
as if a rabbit had been slaughtered there

just before I arrived.
I don't dust anything over it.
I don't jab my boot to shovel any melt.

To the Man Driving I-5
with a Rabbit on His Shoulder

I passed your Chevy Scottsdale on the flats
ahead of Burlington, from the north.
You wore a gray and green plaid jacket,
and one of those mesh ball caps
farmers get skin cancer from. I don't
see too many Scottsdales anymore
without all four tires flat. At my last job,
I used a busted-up red one like a cairn,
turning into the driveway just beyond it.
I was filling boxes then, driving fork.

But the animal on your arm. I thought
it was a retriever pup at first, that hadn't
come into its color. When I came up on the left,
I saw it was a rabbit. A white rabbit,
its curled rhododendron leaf ears swept back
along its trembling spine, shuffling
from one side of your head to the other.

Did you wear it to keep the sun off your neck?
What magic do you know?
I wish you had been driving a little faster.
I would have kept pace with you all afternoon
to see you turn that rabbit into a dove.
It would be one hell of a trick if you hid it
in that see-through hat. I know that's trite,
but it's a trick for the working class
—to make something appear, then take it back.

I could see you were a laborer by the brick dust
on your bumper, and the shovel handles
braced against the cab. If you were

making money on the side with this rabbit,
I don't know. I only knew you
for twenty-five seconds, tops.
Maybe there was a library full of kids
waiting for you at the next exit.
Or you had a roadside stand somewhere,
to indulge your hobby. Selling strawberries, too.
Antiques and finds from the river.
Maybe the little creature was just your companion,
something to talk to on long journeys.

If I hadn't been on the clock,
I could have stayed even with you,
pitching nickels into your truck bed
and cheering. Shown you weren't alone out here.
Then I'd have gotten you to pull over,
us parked right past the rumble strip
at the freeway's edge, so you could saw me in half.
We could have used your black plastic gear box
to do it. I'm big but I could have fit.

Breakfast with My Best Friend, Who Otherwise Fries Eggs for Pay

He says he's going to quit the kitchen
this summer. "It's too hot at the grill
in August anyway and Diamond Jim
is an asshole." He tells me he's got a lead
on a seasonal job trapping maggots
in apple orchards. It's a county gig,
with a vehicle and good benefits.
I tell him *trapping* is a strange word
for *poisoning*, and I really hope
his new insurance will be generous.

Soon our food comes out, and it's time
for our usual. We go through this
whenever we eat out, we who share
one day off per week. I ask him
how my eggs look, how they look
for being over-medium. This morning,
he says the whites are too well done,
and the cook should have used more oil.
"See how it flakes at the edge?"
I say, "Yeah, but they taste just fine."
He tells me I've no eye for eggs, then bites
into his hollandaise-soaked special.

I ask him about my eggs every time,
because I'm fascinated by the devotion,
the authoritative knowledge
given to breakfast food. If I ate meat,
I'm sure he would tell me everything
I wanted to hear about sausage browning,
and maybe even if I didn't,
like the way he has the waitress

recommend the "Meat Lover's Omelet,"
if I eat at his own work on weekends.

Perhaps my friend should quit the kitchen
this summer. It's possible he has gone
as far one can go with America's first meal,
and should give his eye to something grander.
If anybody could develop a foolproof way
to trap apple orchard maggots, it's him.

ROBOTIC DAWNS

Stop lights change as I let them.
My hair is unwashed again. In the morning
the walkers examine the color
of fields in long-sleeve white t-shirts,
and rehydrate themselves with arm-tucked water bottles
like clipboards. My hair unwashed again.

In the morning the walkers. Birds
have been unpackaged; they fly from cartons
of last night's drive-thru excursions. Examine
the color of fields. Bottles like
clipboards. Steam surrounds dogs' bellies.
Arm-tucked. I turn into the machine shop parking lot.

Fields in long-sleeve white t-shirts. Unwashed
again. Fly from last night's drive-thru excursions. Birds have
been unpackaged. The day will click and beep. Chatter. "Which coffee
girl was working?" I turn into the machine. Shop parking lots. In the morning
the walkers surround dogs' bellies. Rehydrate themselves.
Examine the color white. Stop lights change as I let them.

From the Employee Kitchen

The men where I work eat
microwaveable ham and cheese omelets
on top of bumpy sausage patties
between cinnamon-raisin bagel slices,
with butter on all flat surfaces.

Then half of them finish these off
with a smoke in the parking lot,
where their spit splotches the asphalt
like the smashed eyes of clubbed halibut.

It's true every line cook I've ever known
enjoyed a cigarette on break,
but these guys only resemble chefs.
Their aprons are of denim, made thick
to keep metal slag from piercing belly,
with little pockets for calipers,
mechanical pencils, and plastic-capped
miniature blades.

A gunsmith once told me the color
of your collar depended on the hours
of your shift. It's 6:15 on a Thursday
morning, and I am feeling that hue
relies on the quota of calories
in the sandwich you eat to get day done.

THE BLUE COLLAR ARTIST

With safety glasses on,
I have a black plastic unibrow
grown above the shield,
and I imagine myself the Frieda Kahlo
of the machine shop,
and all the low-slung wires on the vertical mill
are monkey's tails
trying to reach my shoulder
for portraits being issued
by security cameras.

My Boss Is a Jewish Carpenter

My only hope is that the driver
of the Lakeside Septic truck,
with its coiled, feces-stained tubes
and its load of metal cylinder
filled with bourgeois shit,
had a sense of humor
when he placed that blue sticker
with bold white letters
on his chrome bumper.

But to suggest Jesus Christ is alive
and well and running a business
in the Greater Seattle Area,
draining crap out of homes
with waterfront views
is too much for one man to reflect on,
waiting to enter the freeway
from a metered ramp at rush hour.
I either need to pull over or out.

Blue Stilly

It's that drive-thru smoke shop
off the highway, with all the old trucks
laboring to maintain idle outside it,
anytime of day. It must do the best
business of anything on the 530,
since the kids at Denny's just get coffee,
and you'd have to be stupid or desperate
to need to stop for gas in a place like this.
It's cheaper either direction, better grade,
and the tanks might even be clean.

Half the population of this burg must be
lined up there, pickups dying and starting
and dying again. It makes me want
to bring my friend Isaac down. He smokes.
It would be worth the fifty-mile drive
to see what the appeal is, to find out
how a drive-thru smoke shop
can keep a stretch of road on its feet.
It's got to send the Shell station business.
The wait looks long enough to call for
more fuel to get home. And maybe
the smokers get hungry for burgers and fries,
or milkshakes, and they stop over
at that Denny's on their way out of town.

I can't even tell what town this is
meant to be. It's too far west
to be Arlington, and I had decided Silvana
existed only on freeway exit signs.
So I'll bring Isaac down here sometime
—take a trip on a Friday night

when he's short on cash and his favorite brand.
It says right on the wall they've got Camels.
Cheap ones, and candy for the kids.
Maybe we'll figure out how,
from a slow queue across the road from it,
the Stilly could ever look blue.

Tavern Woman

She said living now in the single-wide trailer
was fine, "As long as the cat is happy
and the shotgun's dry." She used to go
with a sailor. A merchant marine
who played fast and loose. Easy with money
but wouldn't put a ring on her finger.
Her teeth are all fucked up and her eyes
are crazy. She keeps asking guys
with limp ponytails to arm wrestle. Then loses,
her fist sinking like a doomed vessel.

OVER BREAKFAST

When that rare tourist comes, you tell him
you're not forlorn.
—Richard Hugo

At the Lyman Restaurant and Cocktail Lounge,
I'm reading Richard Hugo while waiting
for my omelet. Then I close the book
and try harder at fitting in. I drink more coffee,
stretch in my seat.

The dish boy wilts in steam. I secretly suspect
the waitress is upset with me
for taking up a whole booth on my own.
The couple at the next table discuss how much
insurance money they might be able to get
for having hit a horse loose in the road.
"I'm starting to feel my neck's been hurt."

Pan fries burst in the kitchen. The smell
of the cross-room counter stools is all
leather and bleach. The drunkard's palm
rides his cheek. On the hill, they're burning
slash piles, the smoke enclosing
this not unappealing diner just off the highway.
Skagit County at morning is a warming griddle.

My overnight hair is a strangle of vines.
No one tells me anything.

II

For the Topless Girls in the Brewery Gulch

With wet fur coats framing naked tits,
you danced in the New Year
on the narrow drive between St. Elmo's Bar
and the Stock Exchange Saloon.
There were three of you. A small posse
in like uniform. Your hair was stuck
to your faces, so when you shook your heads,
the strands tore off strips of foundation.
In the right street light, the negatives
looked like tiger stripes. It was raining.
Tomorrow was a holiday. Everyone knew
this desert water was poison. Of course
you were drunk.

The mariachi band members were done up
as if they had been dug from the graveyard,
with a tuba wrapped around a skeleton,
and a zombie with a green, decaying fist
pulling on a trombone. They had come
out of the club to play on the sidewalk,
elevated three feet above the trench
of the road. Writhing down there,
we were the living dead, clawing from underground.

Your fur coats were getting soaked.
It made them smell more musty, halfway
to rotten. Runoff was threatening
to wash away your high heels. Maybe
that's what happened to your shirts.
Of course you had to be wearing tight
white pants, so when they became stuck

to your asses, your thongs were obvious
from my vantage against a brick wall.

I wasn't single then. I lived with that girl
up the canyon. You all knew her. Small town.
But I'd put her to bed early. Told her
I was going to stay up a little longer
and walked downtown. When I saw
what was waiting for me there,
of course I thought about cheating.
But the giant whitewashed *B*
on the hillside above us, wasn't
for *Beautiful*, because you weren't.
It couldn't have been for *Breasts*,
because soon the cops showed up, and your coats
were buttoned, leaving nothing
but your sternums exposed, shiny with steam
above whatever animals you wore.

The *B* could have been for *Bored*. For me
unloading trucks and working a register,
barely full-time in a grocery store
at the edge of the pit mine. For me, living with someone
who spent all her time in the tub.
But that feeling was really *Discontentment*,
which starts with a *D* and isn't advertised.

It's kept for silence and late nights alone
in crowds. And watching nude girls dance
is all satisfaction and self-loathing.
When the ladies were carted off,
and the band put to rest, I started home.

It was after midnight. The celebration
was over. Postal workers were out
of their uniforms. They wore fringed suede jackets,
and walked beyond the Gulch with painted staffs.

The Unofficial Mayor of Bisbee, Arizona

Hotel managers let him stay in rooms
that were under construction,
when the beds were gone and the walls
reeked of paint. He'd be outside
the Jonquil most October mornings,
smoking and drinking water
from a plastic gallon jug. Dozer
was big as his name, bald on top,
and had a thick black mustache, sharp
against his lip, like a gunslinger's.

Citizens would have him move
furniture and work their yards.
Then they'd take him to the grocery store,
let him buy whatever he wanted.
I saw him choose fresh lemons
and a shaker of salt. Dozer would stuff
his pockets with napkins from the deli,
and walk out the store to the edge
of the pit mine. He'd bisect a lemon
with a compass knife, salt the halves,
and bite into one without making a face,
chewing it, like it was an apple.

The morning I left town I was going to
give him all my booze I'd kept half-full
in the freezer. But Dozer wasn't
on his stoop, and he wasn't
at the gas station, and he wasn't
sleeping in the little courtyard orchard
up the canyon. He wasn't in the tunnel
when I climbed out of the hills,

and there was no ribbon there he'd have
me cut. He wasn't on the highway
to hand me a key, or put a medal
around my neck, and I know
he'd never owned a top hat.

But I remember registering to vote,
and I remember writing him in,
though I was north before I ever read the result.

This Southwestern State

Saying goodbye to a ghost is more final than saying
goodbye to a lover. Even the dead return, but a ghost
once loved, departing will never return.
—Jack Spicer, *After Lorca*

The alien lightning that visited me in Bisbee,
collected like pulsating night clouds
at the summits of the Mule Mountains.
It didn't bring any hard sound, only this
beckoning. And the flashes seemed to go on
longer, lacking thunder break.
As if silence stretches   a thing's term.

I watched them from the front room,
attempting sleep with couch cushions
on the rug with my ringless wife,   needing only
a top-sheet against the monsoon season's heat.

The steel screen door was kept locked
on account of actual aliens.   They shifted
through Tombstone Canyon streets,
stashed in dumpsters and chicken   coops.
Naco and the rest of Old Mexico
were just a short desert run away.

I always get paranoid when I cross that border.
Feel like everybody down there
is in on a secret. Old Mexico   is less a location
than a waylay station, but I am hardly
authority on that stuff.

I helped a Border Patrol agent jump his rig once,
stuck way up in the Huachucas.
He told me he mostly stands in the bushes

and tries to look like a cactus in his green uniform
until somebody happens along.   I happened along.

But I wish I were authority
on this   weather.
How it could be so silent and so   near
—glowing with ocotillo and rock.

What produces this? This ghost   frequency
I'd discovered strictly before midnight
in summer. With my sorrow and inability to write
so well concealed.

I'd have it back. It was   a time.

WHAT I LIKED BEST ABOUT LIVING IN EAST MISSOULA

Those summer nights in Hellgate Canyon
I used to breathe smoke from Lodgepole
Pine wildfires, and admire how no one I knew
could visit me there. Everybody
to the west would only have been allowed
to wait, parked on the interstate
just past Idaho, watching billboards burn
like advertisements for impending madness,
hearing about alternate routes closing by the hour.
Sometimes, sitting on the concrete porch,
I could get a dried urine whiff, off
some methamphetamine trailer down the block,
and that didn't seem too bad a drug,
and Montana didn't seem too poor a place.

THE BUCK

By spring, the headless buck strung upside
-down in my neighbor's cyclone dog pen
is not only lord of the magpies
which feed on frozen strips of flesh
from within the hollow of his ice-cave torso
and cluck while loafing on his bald flanks,
but also over a pair of mule deer doe
long dead, finally unveiled in cold slush.

Each dawn I cannot help the notion
I am incorrectly dressed to be
graveside attendant behind kitchen glass
where I stumble through pots to boil eggs,
no less in my skin than the buck.

To right his winter spent preserving
gutless in a backyard, I almost want
to hire the Mormon family band
that plays traditionals down at the market,
since there are no farmers there this soon
in the year, and those kids look so suited
for death in their blacks and whites,
with doilies at their collars and wrists.

I would have them all sing for the buck,
him in his shit-covered kennel
with his magpies and his harem
and his five-point head dropped in a hole.
Silver-tipped cowboy boots
and runoff. Mandolins and limbs.
I could shoot a short film—see how
in any season at the farmer's market
it wouldn't sell a tape.

INTO DAYS BETWEEN SNOW

When the roads were asphalt again,
and the dusters given different jobs,
I used to step out to the parking lot
with a prep girl for most of her
smoke breaks. The restaurant didn't
schedule those, so during shifts
I eyed her coat hooked nearest the door.

The weather was getting good enough
for full-time habits, but I wasn't
going outside for the cigarettes. I went to stand
beside the curb past the Dumpsters,
to bullshit with her about how she would quit
Missoula and move to Portland.

She said it was temperate enough
in Western Oregon a person could live
under bridges through all seasons,
with easy trains to California if it got
too bad. Her hair had been dyed black
a long time, and there were holes
in the wrists of her favorite hoodie,
so her thumbs could come through.

One night cleaning up, a line cook
told me if as many dicks were poking
out of that girl, as had poked into her,
she would look just like a porcupine.
I listened to the talk, with my rubber
gloves on, then emptied his fryer waste.

By September, she had left Montana,
the Mustard Seed Asian Cafe, and me
a note, giving the little hand-built bench
where she sat to roll sushi. It saved my back,
made it easier to square off a corner
from the rest of the kitchen, while I did
the work that had been passed me.

Until fall, when a few of the galley boys
took it, broke it with hammers,
burned it for their football party.

HOUSE ON COLORADO AVENUE

If the master one day returns, asking
somebody to dust off his hat
and restore his coat to the backside
of the front door, I would do it.
Every breath in this place expands
to the walls, then settles on furniture,
where the carbon monoxide
lapses before being taken in again.

All evening I monitor mold
where it blackens behind the standup
shower stall, and around the border
of the vanity lights.
These window vestibules work
for keeping chill out, but they have made
a swamp of the bedroom linens.
My chest creaks with my sleep.

These one-time servant's quarters
for a destroyed mansion,
hauled close to the river, rented
month-to-month to shoe sellers,
waitresses, an uprooted welder.

And now to me, cross-legged
on carpet listening to the heater
bang on, restringing electric guitars
as fast as the work rusts. Me,
socked-in by rolls of plastic sheeting
sheared into rectangles and taped

over glass. The cabin gasps in fits
from Christmas storms. Each paned
sack of lung rustling to life with wind,
while their good gets measured
in savings on gas bills.

The cord from the hair dryer
used to draw the wrapping tight,
dangles from the bathroom cupboard,
and further up, its shape beckons
a suicide from the dim.

I'd get outside and plead reprieve
from the Chinook, that cold-season
-in-a-canyon lord, but the garbage
hasn't been taken in three weeks,
and the door won't shove open
for weight of trash bags and snow.

What I Could Have Done to East Missoula

Say those summer nights in Hellgate Canyon
I didn't only breathe smoke from Lodgepole
Pine wildfires, but started my own.
Oh, it would be brainless. Those yellow-dry
batteries of timber riding the slope
toward the river could have been reached
only by shot of garden hoses, as flames
shrieked toward single-story houses in blue,
and that playground with the last surviving
merry-go-round in the United States.
Dogs would strain padlocked chains against stakes,
where they yanked backward from the coming heat.
Friends, self-destruction can be put upon
anything, even a highway village met
when I was made of matches, not grass.

PAST THE CASCADES

There are no tickets to that altitude
—Robert Lowell, "Beyond the Alps"

Outside Fishtrap the rain is as much dust
as water, and it dapples parked cars
like gutter spray. Every thirty miles,
the rest stops are full of Pomeranians
and church group busses. Those Seventh Day
Adventists my father stole me from
have finally tracked me down, crowded
into a urinal with one sleeve unrolled.
I swear to them I'd tie my boot
if the clouds didn't make my left wrist ache.

The scrub pines tell me I'm getting higher,
as a hitchhiker says he's looking
to sell a violin. Those spiders behind
the dashboard are dead. Stick your head in
this town and it will come out backward.
The woman I was pressed to this morning
woke me simultaneously with a rooster's call,
asking soft as though her parents
could be home, "Is that a real cock?"

Last night in the mirror of a bar, faces
stopped being real faces. Mustaches grew
legs and ladies' jowls got looser
with each drink. No one was saved.
Not even the hound dug into peanut shells
with its tail warming its nose,
and its owner lost to the bathroom.
It was stepped on at least dozen times
before it was wrestled from its hold
and dragged toward home.

In the Morning It's Evil on the Bedside Table

I kept that spider plant you gave me.
The one you potted yourself
in a washed-out yogurt container.
The one you said would grow
with our kinship. I don't know
what became of the aloe vera
you handed me from the same paper bag.
It must have been lost in a move,
or maybe my mother has it.

The spider plant is still growing.
Often, I let it go brown and wicked,
but it comes back striped and bold
whenever I let it have water
—spreading its greasy leaves over the edges
of the table. Whatever it is strong on,
it isn't love. I feel it planting eggs
in my heart, while its tiny, eye-jammed head
aims downward, feeding off the puss
in my stomach. Its abdomen
plugs my esophagus. Its cable legs
are extended; their fine black hairs are gripped,
along each bone of my ribs.

TRANS WALES

In Snowdonia, shale drags the hillsides down.
Power cables pour rainwater on road brush
where shoulders would be. I'd like to run this car
down a trench and leave it to rust. I'd be lodged somewhere
past the engine but before its trunk—maybe
through the windshield. This morning I woke
in a northern hotel bed. Curtains trembled
behind a newspaper-sealed window. By tonight,
I will be wandering gum-stained Swansea side streets,
watching scholars pee behind chain link fences.
There will be bombed-out castles whispering
to statues everything there is to know
about patience. A sports fan will be kicked
in the gut until he's empty and his rugby jersey
bleeds. Instead, I could be laid-out here, on Snowden
in a rented two-door, as good as a victim, wrecked.

Horse Drawn Boat

I went to buy postcards for my aunt
who waited under a faux-fur hat
at the Esplanade Hotel.
The Atlantic was blossoming
over the plank jetties and brick,
and my head was stuck down my collar,
and within it I was writing.

The words were trimming themselves
from my brain, so I couldn't focus
or see if any of the shops I was passing
were still even open.

But what I was writing
wasn't about looking for postcards
on a winter evening in Wales.
It wasn't about the trip I was taking,
or the language I was hearing,
or the wind, or aunts in faux-fur hats.
That wouldn't come until later.

The writing was about how I dreamed you
in a boat drawn by horses.
And what steel flippers were their new shoes,
eight legs spinning solemn and forbidden
on an uncut sea?

They heaved and steamed
as if it were morning,
except there was no sun.
Fog was the only thing to lighten you.

And weren't you always afraid
of large mammals?

And why did you switch your hair?

But I couldn't ask any of these questions.
The horses had swum away.

Farming in County Sligo, County Leitrim

The boss handed me a blowtorch to change a trailer tire,
said "Use this until I can find a rig to rent."
The lugs were all rust-blistered and the spare
wasn't around, and we wouldn't have had the problem
if he'd only released the brake.

There was a hole the size of my fist where the tire
had been dragged, and there was rain collected
in my hood, so when I thought
to bring it up, I doused myself with water.

The fees were already paid, and the cattle
ready to go, and the mart had already
started, but it had snowed overnight,
and we shouldn't have been driving anyway.

We rented a second rig for way too many euros,
and the guy who drove it tapped me
with his cane every time he laughed.
The cows were loaded up, but we were late
to Drumshanbo, and when we shoved them out
urine splattered our legs.

Some of the paperwork was missing,
so we couldn't sell the calf, so we couldn't
sell the mother either. And we didn't get much
for the old one or the bull, but in the stands
I swear I saw a man eating a chocolate bar
despite the stink.

The auctioneer made the cattle nervous
when they were shot into the pen,

and twice the handler nearly got crushed
before he slipped into the guard. But he kept
whacking them with his switch and letting
the next one through, and hands kept going up,
so I was chicken to scratch my head.

That night I took out the English girl again,
but she wouldn't come inside, and we talked
in her tiny car until I wished
I'd been castrated. The Lake Isle of Innisfree
was just a tuft of grass, and Doony
just a rock, and that damn Alsatian
snarled at me every time I went near the house.
So I took another bath in the out-building
with a rag in the sink.

PIEBALD BIRTH ON JOSIE'S MAKESHIFT FARM

He went into the vagina with a fistful
of orange bailing twine, and fished around
for awhile, up to his elbows
in chunky blood, until he had it good
and knotted on the back legs of the lamb.

Those back legs came out easy enough,
stemming from the uncurling winter wool
of the ewe, like insect antennae
out from a cocoon. But the torso
was well lodged, anchored
in the trembling uterus, still but stubborn.

It was dark inside the stone shed,
and the ewe was black already.
She slumped in the corner like lightning,
which is to say she could only be seen
in glimpses, but made unsettling noise.

Her breath steamed with her blood
as she bellowed and cooed
in the morning cold. The farmer
braced his boot against the upturned bottom
of a bucket, as he began to yank
in earnest. He appeared concerned,

but full of duty, with the white sunlight
that had started to make it through
the shed windows, turning the dim fluorescent.
For a little while, the place wasn't
ramshackle, wasn't an abandoned

storage space off a forgotten tennis court
covered with sheep shit. It was an institution,
with shovels and hoes leaned outside
the structure like orderlies with no clue
where their hands had gone, and no idea
what should have been sanitized.

After half a dozen more heaves,
the lamb popped free of the womb, and hung
from the bailing twine, filled with silence.
It was black like its mother, but with white
splotches on its flanks and chest.

Or, with splotches that could become white
if they were washed. For now,
they were pink and creamy, and provided
a swirled effect as their vessel was spun
in circles over the cobbled shed floor.
The ewe collapsed into a clump of hay.

Every few rotations, the farmer would halt
with a jerk, to check if the lamb was breathing,
but once he had done this several minutes,
and he himself could hardly stand
for dizziness, he stopped altogether.

He raised his tweed blue arm
until the lamb's downturned head was even
with his eyes, and the body was gently unwinding
some in air. When it stopped
and only swayed, the farmer spat,
then slung the body against the shed wall.

It dropped with a slap on the stones.
Just as the farmer turned for the door,
the lamb raised its head from the mess of itself
and let go a short, gargled bleat—awake now,
punched with enough air to live awhile.

They Couldn't Even Kill Their Television

When you asked me to marry, all you gave
was a cell phone ring. Well, honey, you know
I'm off the grid, like that couple we knew
with zero percent body fat, living
on the desert, near the border crossing
at Agua Prieta. But I don't have
a Prince Albert piercing, or corked earlobes.
My hair will not bind if I don't wash it.

So, no, I don't want to be sequestered
to the new age dream you were somehow taught
by your mother, from her North Idaho
fortress, with a fence around the garden,
and never enough split wood in the shed.

Sometimes I think of your poor stepfather
running up and down the carpeted stairs
at every one of his commercial breaks,
with socks on his feet at all times, to hide
his fungal toenails. And his teeth had gone
feral, and his eyes turned laser blue.

I Went in with My Hands Up

Sweet Jesus at morning the queenly women of our youth!
The monumental creatures of our summer lust!
—Thomas McGrath, *Letter To An Imaginary Friend*

It was a little like that pregnant black heifer
stuck in the aluminum feeder-box
sized specifically for calves—jackknifed,
full on muesli and seed, her head turned out
toward the snowy morning.

Me and that 80-year-old Irishman
had to lift it, the several hundred pounds
of green metal, knowing, with our elbows
hefted above our divergent hairlines,
and our ankles foundered in thick pasture mud,
we would be totally exposed.

And she'd be coming out in a hurry,
big and taut around the middle.
Us just hoping she wouldn't lose
her calf in the fuss.

It was a little like that. Stopping by
that girl's house the other night.
Except without the help. And this doesn't
come out right. I would never
be so pigheaded as to compare a woman
to a cow. Just to compare the *parameters*
using the inconsequential vessel of simile.

I didn't even know what horns
that heifer bore. What spawn
might be brewing within her black belly.
But it had to be done. She had to be

turned loose. I kept my legs. And one
doesn't count as a stampede.

Beasts and Violins

I wandered the house looking for a blank notebook
today, until I found one of the small spiral ones
I prefer. It had tacky shots of mountain climbers
on the cover, and read *Dig In!* with bright letters.
I don't prefer the styling, but appreciate the portability.
And though it was in my house, the notebook
wasn't mine, and wasn't empty.

Inside it had lists. Lists of bands, places, problems
—with notes detailing why my ex-girlfriend was unhappy.
My name appeared on most pages. It was hers,
left on a bookshelf for over one year.
She always kept lists, as if her life could be categorized
into columns of good and bad, written repeatedly
like an incantation, banishment spell, or scale.

There was a section detailing which albums
were best of the year, another with her all-time favorite
movies. One more with the pros and cons
of her parents, and a paragraph on how
I was controlling and didn't care. There was a travelogue
of notable locations in the desert southwest,
filled out with names of people we had known
in a little town. I even found some suggestions
that, by now, she was only with me for the dogs.

Still, it was only a quarter full of this shit,
and I wanted the notebook. So I ripped out her pages,
stuck them in the winter fire. The flames made me
happy. Filled me up, like I was drunk
in a train car lounge, and every time I checked my wallet,
I would find another twenty. Maybe there

would be weeper country music playing
and I'd be hoping the fiddle would take the melody,

and in the last thirty seconds, it would.
The suspense would all be worth it. The heartache
would become transcendent. I'd jump
off my stool and dance right there on the train.
The snow would be too high for the wolves
to give chase. Their eyes would cut tree limbs
as they raised their heads to howl.

Camping with Mad, Far from Montana

She comes from the lake steaming
like a logging truck at dawn.
She's thick. All muscle and belly.
Her head is a little too small for her body.
There's a black spot on her back,
a saddle for a dwarf cowboy,
but she wouldn't let anyone ride.
She hates guests more than I do.

Her side has healed where she was mauled
by the loose Rottweiler in Missoula,
almost a year ago. Silver fur
has covered the scars left by entry points
of the drainage tube I cleaned
by the hour for three days,
to see how she would recover.
I fed her chicken and rice and slept
some beside her.

She peed down my chest,
before, when I hefted her
from the after hours vet's office,
drowsy with drug,
her cattle dog tongue dangling
over my shoulder. It wasn't
like carrying a child to bed.
No, it wasn't like that at all.
It was like lifting myself

from that town. From the charmless
job rolling sushi in a casino restaurant
and the indifferent girlfriend.

Lifting myself from the oncoming
winter and weather inversions
that clogged Big Sky Country
for weeks with wood-smoked, diesel sickness.

At night by the campfire, Maddy sits
just outside the light, whiffing
the dark. She rises at the rustle
of leaves. A cougar would kill her.
Rip her apart the way no Rottweiler
could. But every good dog
needs a chore. I imagine she's only
trying to square the deal.

Now That the Brown Pelicans Have Flown Elsewhere

it's another season teaching children
how to hunt freshwater clams with their feet
and losing my best jewelry to the lake.
I have come to admit Alaska
will never be a future, just an escape.
That Great Northern Pike would've taken
half my fingers if I hadn't let it swim.

The women here only trouble my sleep.
I dream they live alone in my house,
while I watch them from outside the window
on all fours. Still, they wear negligees
like they expect me, leave jars of milk
aging unchecked on the counter.

I would like to remain on the delta
smelling forever what seals have killed.
I would also like very much to stop
poisoning their best meats.

When it's evening and the nets are in
and the cafes fill with conversation
I am not privy to, I think on how
things might have come out if the dog
hadn't warned me of that black bull
standing sideways on the highway,
with its color just another section
of night, and me powering toward it
dumb as he but with no horns.

I might never have gotten to taste
that bucket of restaurant-ready pickles
my best friend got on the cheap after his boss
forgot to have them arrive pre-sliced.
They were the only food in the fridge
for weeks, and we fished deep into that brine
during darts and after drinking.
They were all we ate, all we could hold.

All the same it made our hands cold
to feel for the bottom that way.
Just like Brown Pelicans off course
and their barnacled posts, wandering in a region
more brutal than they are built for,
with their pouches hauling ice cannonballs
and their feathers useless for camouflage.

THE PARANOID

He drew me with flowers: purple and red
carnations set in two ribbed jugs of lake
water, beside a rock on a moss bed.
I saw them from the road, hardly awake
and looking for a site. I pressed the brake.
Greeny debris drifted below the stems.
The blossoms were fresh. They were not fake.
I thought they'd been placed by a gentleman.
Someone wooing a girl the way they did back when.

I got a fire going, fed the dogs meat
—moved the carnations on top of a stump.
I heated soup and chose a log for seat.
When the moon came up, it rose like a lump
on the night sky. A pale white tumor sunk
into black. I'd started reading a book.
The dogs were asleep and I could smell skunk
drifting down the mountain. I took a look
with a flashlight through the thin trees, but nothing shook.

Midnight, when my big dog growled, she was late.
I woke enough to feel my spine severed
by the ax swung strong in my back. Fish bait
stank on the handle. I hadn't heard
him. He'd come up from the lake, a night bird
between the pines, lifting his hide boots slow.
Tipping from the log, I spoke a ghost's words:
"He carries death and he carries it low.
He plants flowers in water where you're sure to go."

III

BELLINGHAM'S FAVORITE SON

Night in town is framed by the black hole
of my hood. The surviving solar ring
to my face's eclipsing moon. The bowl
my beard floats in. The reason owls don't sing.

I see the State Street drunks through the hollow
of a tree. Tell them, "Tonight I can't spare
a thing." The dealers on Railroad follow
cop cars with curses, but the whores just stare.

Down the block I still get peanuts for free.
The college kids pay for the locals' perks.
Wall guitars hang, missing strings like teeth,
and I fix them. It never feels like work.

When GP mercury kills all of us
will neon still burn? You all know I've tried
to leave, but water cannot haul a bus.
I am brought back by each winter's high tide,

slumped over on the beach, wondering how
much tighter I could have clung to the bow.

Beast in Me

When I said I would take you swimming,
I meant we would drive out
to the reservation and I'd say
it was too cold to take our clothes off.

When I said I would take you camping,
I meant I would wait until you went
away to Spain, then go to the hills by myself.

When I said "Yes, I will definitely be
at that show," I meant I would
show up late, with a can of Rainier
in each of my pants pockets,
then leave once they were empty.

When I said we should maybe just
keep this friendly, I meant
I wouldn't be calling you again.

And when you reported all this
to my best friend, he agreed with you
I was unkind, and listened
while you complained
two hours on the bar bench.

Honey, I was only a few blocks away,
putting the moves on someone new.

What All Foxes Know
(Two Ways Out of Their Burrows)

In the apartment night, my friend smokes
in his robe and further ruins the air
with oil lamps. I squat by the sewing machine
that shot through his great aunt's finger
and read his essay. The bag is tied
about the tea cup's handle, and this

would have all seemed quite civilized
had we been in a field tent on the eve
of battle with Yanks, instead
of a ramshackle building down the hill
from a college neither of us attends.

Winter gusts blow my Stonewall beard back
through the single-paned, second-story
window. My friend tucks up his violin
and begins tightening the bow. By the end
of the essay, he's misspelled "cigarette."

Teaching the Beasts

There are rabbits in the industrial district,
this place where wild meets the workforce
as cities expand and want flat space
for large buildings, parking lots, and men.
I watch them beyond the bay door, myself
strapped to a CAD machine forever
on its rails and pulling me toward another
sunset. The pavement out there is no better

than tundra in winter, but these creatures
have forged homes from landscaped shrubbery
and hills of dirt where a warehouse will be
by the month's end. They skitter
on their errands of food, hustling backward
as much as they progress, beneath diesel rigs.
And the trucks with dual stacks do look
like owls descended from a grander place.

When my machine runs a long cycle
and is cutting good parts, I let the dog
down from the Ford and loose her
on the rabbits. She is too slow and old
to catch them, with teeth kibble
hasn't kept fresh, so I don't think of myself
as inhumane to let this hunt
go on. I think of it as teaching a pet,
while it breaks through pallet stacks and brush,
it mustn't always behave like a child.
And I am letting fiercer animals know
they ought not be comfortable parasites.

Myself, I never learn anything more than panic
and the endless rebellion of both
rodents and expensive machinery.
When I make it back to the shop,
with nothing like meat to show for winnings,
I see the mice have been at my supper
and the cutter is off-track and spraying sparks
over the concrete as if it could burn.

Small Engines

The wolf at my door turned out
not to be a wolf, but a skunk-sprayed dog
scrambling blind across the porch,
and bashing itself into the chicken wire fence
like a salmon against a seine.

The air outside was too full with funk
to even register scent, so I watched
the beast awhile from behind the screen door,
assuming it had been shot. It was a pit bull.
I didn't do anything fast.

Soon, I also was sick with the smell
and nearly puked on my slippers.
It reeked like getting swallowed
into a toxic bog, or being breathed on
by some fantastic, moon-born troll.

From the front gate I signaled the dog
with clicks and short whistles,
so I could let him go out into the night.
He was ready to be turned loose
into the misery he was due.

I would have done the same for an actual wolf,
be she with a clamped leg in the woods,
or locked into one of those bear crates
people keep at roadside stands with kart tracks
and plank mazes near Glacier Park.

The dog wandered blind toward streetlights
as I turned back to the house,
leaving the gate swinging at the dark
for the skunk that must have burrowed itself
into the dead leaves beneath the deck.

The reek that made it in through the door
kept me six hours from sleep,
and by morning my head was ruined
as I set to work securing the fence
with cinder block and straightened iron posts.

IN A TWILIGHT TOWN

At these hours a girl shows me the scar
she earned after her father's chainsaw
bucked against her calf while he evened
the backyard stumps. "It cut clear to my meat,"
she says. "They had to fly me to the city."
The rough, shiny lump is not grotesque.
Her leg has grown around the wound
same as how trees will hatchet strikes.

She still wears skirts, for now, because
her body won't be a woman's for a few
more years, and free magazine offers
don't come this far out in the country.
The bald slice through one eyebrow is either
from barbed wire or dog. Could have
been her brother, before they sent him
to that school for boys just like him.

I'd like to hear about all those goldfish
that never survived through winter
on her parents' porch. I'd like to know how
the couch felt when it froze through.
But the plane for the mail route is spinning on
and this place will always be her stop.
The night makes us all older, and just walking
toward it, she covers her thighs with the dark.

An Upstream Tow for an Early Date

Because I cannot tie one knot well
I tie several, and that's how it was
in Oregon, launching off that rotten dock
with the birds in the brush oblivious
to their names and the river rocks
the look of brown trout spotted by shade.

I tried to call the smell of the water.
It was mineral mostly, with algae
that had grown sweet as cheese.
The scent was as much from the oaks.
Their stinking roots along the bank
made the whole scene fecund, sexy
—like a body had been hidden somewhere.

My kayak hauled its rented mate behind,
bearing a girl, strange in a straw hat.
Had we harsher personalities,
it could have become that folk song.
The trip would have been traditional
if I'd left her dead in the weeds,
forever refusing to wed, while I
sulked homeward weeping for mother.

Except I was paddling against the flow
and it was too hot to think of murder
or the possibility of marriage,
or any tune better than the water beat.
The girl was harming nothing
but my arms, which are muscled
only as weight allows, and screamed
with blood each time the line jerked taut.

AT THE DEDICATION

I didn't know how to say to the crowd
I hardly knew the man. I was just shy
of five when he died, and remember him
the way most children remember
their early-deceased uncles, through a line
of untied images. Him on a slow climb
from his Mercedes, sporting black gloves.
Him standing with strained posture
on the deck of some stairs, hair gone
transparent from treatment, and a face
pleased by afternoon sun. I also recall
flying a gull feather down his plot
—it, just behind the descending casket.

How could I tell them that was all
I could share? The crowd was a night
full of knuckled raccoon hands, scraping
for crayfish and still-meaty bones
in the Clatskanie River, just outside
the banquet hall glass. And Christ
they were kind, offering cheese,
and orange punch, and rum cake,
and two nights at an inn, and Cub Scouts
holding stiff flags at the ceremony
the next day. What could I give them back?

I am no ambassador to the dead,
no dignitary worthy of write-offs.
That was the first time I had ever touched
a mayor. I wanted to say to her:
"The only ghosts I know are still living.
One squats on the hill above my house,

drinking wine, surrounded by swords
and stuffed animals. Two more sleep alone.
This uncle you've bought me to speak for,
I'm no authority on him."

Except she was wearing all pink and pearls,
and wouldn't have understood.
So I did my best to look well-dressed,
commanded the podium. Tried to be charming.

LORD OF SPORES

Of all the things I've stolen from outside
houses left abandoned in the woods,
it isn't the rusted wagon wheels or bull skulls
I admire most. It's the mushrooms
lifted from the edges of runoff trenches
and mounds of sod topping septic tanks.

Fungus clings to these lost places
same as it does burn zones and gullies,
as if the organism truly were of one
great mind, like the kraken in his sea,
and had learned to communicate with vacancy,
to figure where it ought to send sprouts next.

I pull them, let them drop to a cloth bag.
I fry them with flour and spice
or stir them with a boil of nettles.

If a corpse ever observed my approach
from a chair beside a second floor window,
hissing all alone like a toilet will,
let its rot speak to that great mind of how
delicately I stepped on the moss,
and of how there is nothing to me
that won't someday be bound with it.

A Morning at *Adrift*

I can't put "toothbrushes" into a poem, I really can't . . .
—Sylvia Plath

In the cafe, a woman takes pictures
of her orange juice, while I try
to find a good way to force *toothbrushes*
into a poem. Suddenly it's done

so I go back to my beans, watching the lady
switching lenses and switching angles,
without having even sipped from her muse
whereas I brushed soon as I showered.

I could never ask the woman
why she wastes her juice's sweetness
on photography, or why it seems
half my writing gets set at breakfast.

She would probably think it strange
to put so many things of zero consequence
into clumsy verse with no rhyme
when rain is going on outside, and gulls.

FIXED BEASTS

Say in Vantage we stop for breakfast
across the river from the Wild Horse
Monument. And I'll feel bad
finishing my two-egg special
staring at the bulb-gut of the lone man
hunched at the table near us
where it globes out from his sweatshirt hem
with gray hairs for cloud cover.

But you and I will sit on the same side
of the booth, like any good pair.
I'll drink half your coffee, all
my juice. We'll talk of what time
we're making, and of how I'd like
a mechanical pie display in the library
of the home we'll own someday.

When we leave the cafe, and I slow
in my rig to take that turn
into the high country on Interstate 90,
I'll get fat listening to you
blowing your Belcanto, that pink
harmonica from Italy I bought
in Ireland, before we'd even met.

Then you, with your master's thesis
on-file at the University of Oregon,
with its title of *Why I Hate Horses*,
will explain: "Sometimes a harmonica
can sound like it has two people playing it.
Or one person and a horse."

HEART LAKE: OR,
POEM FOR THE MISTAKEN BOY

At Heart Lake, some fucking kid shouts at me
he's been gutting fish where I swim, and asks
if I like swimming in "dead fish guts."
He's fat like me, with longish hair.
Beside me in the water, my girlfriend turns
and asks what that little girl on shore is saying.
I think, *Shit, it's going to be at least a decade*
before this boy can develop a reasonable beard
—someone should at least get him to trim his hair.
But it won't be me. I don't have the heart
to teach the boy what I had to learn.
I'm too shocked with the thought
that twelve years ago, when I was proud
with a ponytail, and even tubbier than now,
the woman I love might have seen me
as less than all male. So my comeback is limp.
I yell, "Saying *dead fish guts* is redundant."
"The killing," I shout, "is implied."

THE FAIR *Kaleetan,*
BETWEEN FRIDAY HARBORAND ANACORTES

On the ferry, the Pakistanis are all sleeping
on each other's denim shoulders.
Their mustaches riffle upwards,
as their faces roll toward the ceiling.
In the aisle, kids play Red Light/Green Light,
until the youngest starts to fuss,
and our vessel rumbles over another log
as if it were practicing for time trials
at the county fair. From the booth beside,
I realize I've never known the difference
between Mandarin and Cantonese,
but I'm not made uneasy by the staring baby.

I've got a girl on my chest, where there hasn't
been one for years. My wrist is braced
against her unconscious skull
so I can write this down. I'm wondering how
it came to this--being sandwiched
between foreigners, a losing child,
and the San Juan Islands, in a region
I call home, but have hardly explored. How I made it
onto this mobile tunnel for cars
this late in my youth, when I finally feel proud
to be the only one awake and scribbling poetry.

She rustles whenever I mark a period,
The Chinese family begins a countdown from twenty-five
in English. The late-set sun reminds me
it isn't New Year's Eve,
and these strangely solitary blots of firs
are a long ways from Cape Canaveral.
As they ease into the single-digits,

I start to think it is the countdown
for when my heart will stop, but at least
they sound joyful about it. I whisper
for my girl's brain tumor to be kind to her
while I wait to see what will come with *zero*.

SPOOKY PORTRAIT

For your late-October birthday, I've framed
the black pencil sketch that girl did
of you and me at the downtown October art show.
I placed it in the fanciest frame I could find
from one of those discount overstock stores
Canadians have ruined for the rest of us.
It has plastic pearls on all corners and is made
of milky green glass, with accents
in metal lace patterns. It cost six dollars.
A dollar more than the picture it would hold.
With a compass knife, I carved a mat
from cardboard stock, decorated it with purple
drawings of human limbs and eye balls,
then assembled everything and wrapped it in newspaper.

This was all an enjoyable task, which I considered
fitting for the sketch. That haunted sketch
with me in a turban, and a beard
more angular than the one I wear.
You, one eye twice the diameter of the other,
a smile stretched and curling with your hair.
Both of us in ornate clothing. Also
the skeleton baby between. It should have
seemed presumptuous to bestow such a death
on a pair of youthful lovers, but here we welcomed
the little skull and bones. You stroked it.
I had a bottle for feeding in my right breast pocket.
Though the portrait couldn't show
what the bottle was filled by, I'll tell you now
it was steaming red candle wax.

BIOGRAPHICAL NOTE

Caleb Barber lives in Bellingham, Washington, where he works days at an aerospace machine shop. He earned a BA from Western Washington University in English and creative writing, and received an MFA in poetry from the Northwest Institute of Literary Arts off of Whidbey Island. He has been widely published in literary magazines, most notably with a feature in *Poet Lore*. The title poem of this book appeared in *Best American Poetry 2009*.